Soccer Passing & Receiving:

A Step-by-Step Guide on How to Work with Your Teammates

Dylan Joseph

Soccer Passing & Receiving: A Step-by-Step Guide on How
to Work with Your Teammates
By: Dylan Joseph
©2018

Bonus!

Wouldn't it be nice to have the steps in this book on an easy 1-page printout for you to take to the field? Well, here is your chance!

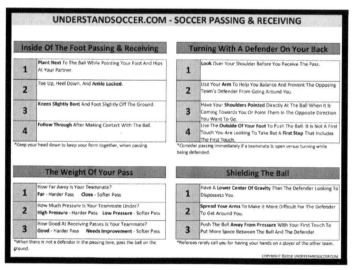

UNDERSTANDSOCCER.COM - SOCCER PASSING & RECEIVING

Inside Of The Foot Passing & Receiving

1	**Plant Next** To The Ball While Pointing Your Foot And Hips At Your Partner.
2	Toe Up, Heel Down, And **Ankle Locked.**
3	**Knees Slightly Bent** And Foot Slightly Off The Ground.
4	**Follow Through** After Making Contact With The Ball.

*Keep your head down to keep your form together, when passing.

Turning With A Defender On Your Back

1	Look Over Your Shoulder Before You Receive The Pass.
2	Use Your **Arm** To Help You Balance And Prevent The Opposing Team's Defender From Going Around You.
3	Have Your **Shoulders Pointed** Directly At The Ball When It Is Coming Towards You Or Point Them In The Opposite Direction You Want To Go.
4	Use The **Outside Of Your Foot** To Push The Ball. It Is Not A First Touch You Are Looking To Take But A **First Step** That Includes The First Touch.

*Consider passing immediately if a teammate is open versus turning while being defended.

The Weight Of Your Pass

1	How Far Away Is Your Teammate? **Far** - Harder Pass **Close** - Softer Pass
2	How Much Pressure Is Your Teammate Under? **High Pressure** - Harder Pass **Low Pressure** - Softer Pass
3	How Good At Receiving Passes Is Your Teammate? **Good** - Harder Pass **Needs Improvement** - Softer Pass

*When there is not a defender in the passing lane, pass the ball on the ground.

Shielding The Ball

1	Have A **Lower Center Of Gravity** Than The Defender Looking To Dispossess You.
2	**Spread Your Arms** To Make It More Difficult For The Defender To Get Around You.
3	Push The Ball **Away** From Pressure With Your First Touch To Put More Space Between The Ball And The Defender

*Referees rarely call you for having your hands on a player of the other team.

COPYRIGHT ©2018 UNDERSTANDSOCCER.COM

Go to this Link for an **Instant** 1-Page Printout: UnderstandSoccer.com/free-printout

This FREE guide is simply a "Thank You" for purchasing this book. This 1-page printout will ensure that the knowledge you obtain from this book makes it to the field.

Table of Contents

About the Author

There I was, a soccer player who had difficulties scoring. I wanted to be the best on the field but lacked the confidence and know-how to make my goal a reality. Every day, I dreamed about improving, but the average coaching and my lack of knowledge only left me feeling alone and like I couldn't attain my goal. I was a quiet player and my performance often went unnoticed.

This all changed after my junior year on the Varsity soccer team of one of the largest high schools in the state. During the team and parent banquet at the end of the season, my coach decided to say something nice about each player. When it came to my turn to receive praise, the only thing he came up with was that I had scored two goals that season even though it was against a lousy team, so they didn't really count...

It was a very painful statement that after the 20+ game season, all that could be said of my efforts were two goals that didn't count. Since that moment, I have been forever changed considering one of my greatest fears came true; I was called out in front of my family and friends. Because of that, I got serious. With a new soccer mentor, I focused on the training to obtain the skills to build my confidence and become the goal scorer I always dreamed of being. The next season, after just a few months, I found myself moved up to the starting position of center midfielder and scored my first goal of the 26 game season in only the third game.

I kept up the additional training led by a proven goal scorer to build my knowledge. Fast forward to present day and as a result of the work and focus on the skills necessary, I figured out how to become a goal scorer who averages about two goals and an assist per game, all because of an increase in my understanding of how to play soccer. I was able to take my game from bench-warmer who was called out in front of everybody to the most confident player on the field.

Currently, I am a soccer trainer in Michigan working for Next Level Training. I advanced through their rigorous program as a soccer player and was hired as a trainer. This program has allowed me to guide world-class soccer players for over a decade. I train soccer players in formats ranging from one-hour classes to weeklong camps and from instructing groups of 30 soccer players all the way down to working one-on-one with individuals looking to play for the United States National Team. If you live in the Metro Detroit and want to be the best player in the league, Next Level Training is for you. Learn more at www.next-leveltraining.com.

Additional Books by the Author that are Available on Amazon:

Soccer Training: A Step-by-Step Guide on 14 Topics for Intelligent Soccer Players, Coaches, and Parents

Soccer Shooting & Finishing: A Step-by-Step Guide on How to Score

Soccer Dribbling & Foot Skills: A Step-by-Step Guide on How to Dribble Past the Other Team

Dedication

This book is dedicated to all the soccer players, coaches, and parents who are reading this information to increase their confidence, their players' knowledge, and their child's self-esteem to pass around the other team to score 10 times (10X) more goals. It was not too long ago that I was a struggling defensive center midfielder who lacked the confidence to play a pass with one-touch and did not know how to receive a pass in a way that created tons space for me. After obtaining the knowledge and implementing it successfully, it is very realistic for me to score five goals in two games. This statement is not to boast or impress you, but to express that with the correct techniques, you can effectively pass around the other team and increase the number of goals you score too.

Also, this book is dedicated to my soccer friends. Antonio Denkovski, Anxhelo Gegprifti, Carlos Solorio, Chris Wolowski, Jasko Jusic, Kevin Solorio, Nabil Awkal, Samer Awkal, Toni Sinistaj, Tom Catalano, and Youssef Hodroj. These guys have been great teammates and friends over the years. They are always up for passing me the ball and down to tell me when I make a mistake. These are a high-quality group of guys that much of the material in this book and other books have been tested with and against. Furthermore, I greatly appreciate their insights on how to make the books in this Understand Soccer series better.

Preface

The title of this book is *Soccer Passing & Receiving*. Average soccer players consider a pass that travels to their teammate a success. Great soccer players know where to pass the ball to make it as easy for their teammate as possible. This book dives deep into how to pass the ball correctly and the keys to receive the ball with ease. This book gives you the tips, tricks, tweaks, and techniques to become the person on your team that can consistently pass around the other team.

This book will help you become the most admired player on your team. Understand that changing one or two things may help improve your game, but once you start implementing most, if not all of the techniques described in this book, you will see a significant improvement in your performance on the field. The knowledge in this book is only helpful when applied. Therefore, apply it to be sure you are dribbling in the appropriate situations by using the most effective and easiest to understand skills to score 10X more goals each season. 10X more goals each season will lead to several more wins every season for your team. For any words that you are unsure of the meaning, please reference the index in the back of the book.

INDIVIDUAL SOCCER PLAYER'S PYRAMID

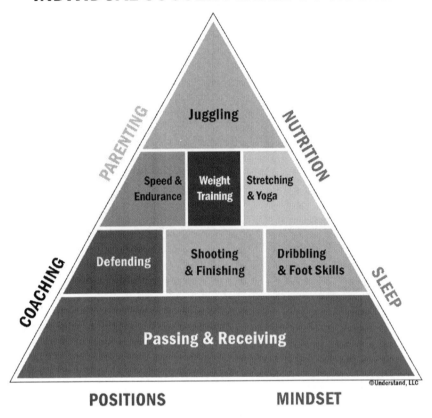

If you are looking to improve your skills, your child's confidence, or your players' abilities, it is essential to understand where dribbling & foot skills play into the bigger picture of developing a soccer player. In the image above, you can see that the most critical field-specific things to work on are at the base of the Individual Soccer Player's Pyramid. Note: A team's pyramid may look slightly different based on the tactics the players can handle and the approach the coach decides to use for games. The pyramid is a quality outline when you are looking to improve an individual soccer player's game. All of the elements in the pyramid and the items surrounding it play a meaningful part in becoming a better player, but certain things should be read and mastered first before moving on to other topics.

You will notice that passing & receiving is at the foundation of the pyramid because if you can receive a pass and make a pass in soccer, you will be a useful teammate. Though you may not be the one that is consistently scoring, the person that is dispossessing the other team, or the player that can dribble through several opponents, you will have the fundamental tools needed to play the sport and contribute to your team.

As you move one layer up, you find yourself with a decision to make on how to progress. Specifically, the pyramid is created with you in mind because each soccer player and each soccer position has different needs. Therefore, your choice regarding which path to take first is dictated by the position you play and more importantly, by the position that you want to play. In soccer and life, just because you are in a particular spot, position, or even a job, it does not mean that you have to stay there forever if that is not your choice. However, it is not recommend to refuse playing a position if you are not in the exact role you want, as it takes time to develop the skills that will allow you to make a shift from one position to another.

If you are a forward or if you want to become one, then consider your route on the second layer of the pyramid to start with shooting & finishing. As your abilities to shoot increase, your coach will notice your new finishing skills and be more likely to move you up the field if you are not a forward already. Be sure to communicate to the coach that you desire to be moved up the field to a more offensive position, which will increase your chances as well. If you are already a forward, then dive deep into this topic to ensure you become the leading scorer on your team and in the entire league. Notice that shooting & finishing is considered less critical than passing & receiving because you have to pass the ball up the field before you can even take a shot on net.

Otherwise, you can start by progressing to dribbling & foot skills from passing & receiving because the proper technique is crucial to dribble the ball well. It is often necessary for a soccer player to use a skill to protect the ball from the other team or to advance the ball up the field to place their team in a favorable situation to score. The selection of this route immediately following passing &

receiving is often taken first by midfielders and occasionally by forwards.

Defending is another option of how you can proceed from passing & receiving. Being able to keep the other team off the scoreboard is not an easy task. Developing a defender's mindset, learning which way to push a forward, understanding how to position your body, knowing when to foul, and using the correct form for headers is critical to a defender on the back line looking to prevent goals.

Finish all three areas in the second layer of the pyramid before progressing up the pyramid. Dribbling and defending the ball (not just shooting) are useful for an attacker, shooting and defending (not just dribbling) are helpful for a midfielder, while shooting and dribbling (not just defending) are helpful for a defender. Having a well-rounded knowledge of the skills needed for the different positions is important for all soccer players. It is especially essential for those soccer players looking to change positions in the future. Shooting & finishing, dribbling & foot skills, and defending are oftentimes more beneficial to learn first for soccer players than the next tier of the pyramid, so focus on these before spending time on areas higher up in the pyramid. In addition, reading about each of these areas will help you to understand what your opponent wants to do as well.

Next, once you have improved your skills at the 1st and 2nd tiers of the pyramid, move upwards to fitness. As you practice everything below this category on the pyramid, your fitness and strength will naturally increase. It is difficult to go through a passing/dribbling/finishing drill for a few minutes without being out of breath. Performing the technical drills allows soccer players to increase their fitness naturally. This reduces the need to focus exclusively on running for fitness. Coming from a soccer player and trainer (someone with a view from both sides), I know that a constant focus on running is not as fulfilling and does not create long-lasting improvements. Whereas, emphasizing the shooting capabilities, foot skills, and defending knowledge of a soccer player does create long-lasting change. Oftentimes, the coaches that focus on running their players in practice are the coaches that care to improve their team but have limited knowledge of many of the soccer-specific topics that would quickly increase their players' abilities. Not only does fitness in soccer include your endurance, but it also addresses your ability to run with agility and speed, develop strength and power, while improving your flexibility through stretching and yoga to become a well-rounded soccer player.

Similarly to the tier below it, you should focus on the fitness areas that will help you specifically, while keeping all of the topics in mind. For example, you may be a smaller soccer player that could use some size. Then, you would consider emphasizing weight training to gain the much-needed muscle to avoid being pushed off the ball. However, you would still want to stretch before and after a lifting workout or soccer practice/game to ensure that you stay limber and flexible, so that you can recover quickly and avoid injuries.

Maybe you are a soccer player in your 20s, 30s, or 40s. Then, emphasizing your flexibility and practicing a bit of yoga would do a world of good to ensure you keep playing soccer for many more years. However, doing a few sets of push-ups, pull-ups, squats, lunges, sit-ups, etc. per week will help you maintain or gain a desirable physique.

Furthermore, you could be in the prime of your career in high school, college, or at a pro level, which would mean that obtaining the stamina and endurance to run for 90+ minutes is the most essential key to continue pursuing your soccer aspirations.

Finally, we travel to the top of the pyramid, which includes juggling. Juggling the soccer ball is something fun to practice in your own free time away from the field or when you are standing in line and waiting to start a drill. It will certainly help with your first touch, but there are more important things to develop during an individual's or team's practice. A general recommendation is that when you can juggle the ball 50 times in a row or more with your feet, continuing to work on juggling will not provide huge increases in your performance. Therefore, use juggling as a way to fill otherwise unproductive time in training or during free time to more quickly become a great soccer player. The importance of juggling is explained in more detail in the first book of the series - *Soccer Training: A Step-by-Step Guide on 14 Topics for Intelligent Soccer Players, Coaches, and Parents*, in addition to a whole host of other critical topics you need to know as a soccer player, coach, or parent.

If you have not read *Soccer Training: A Step-by-Step Guide*, it is highly recommend you do in order to gain in-depth knowledge of many of the crucial topics within the areas of the pyramid. Furthermore, there are a few soccer terms that are described in detail in the Soccer Training book that may only be referenced in this book. Picking up a copy of the book will act as a good gauge to see how much you know about each topic. This will help to determine if a book later in the series written about a different subject in the soccer pyramid will be beneficial for you.

The last portion of the pyramid are all the areas that surround the pyramid. Though these are not skills and subjects that can be addressed by your physical abilities, they each play key roles in rounding out the complete soccer player. For example, a young soccer player with a supportive parent/guardian or two is beneficial for transporting the child to games, providing the equipment needed, the fees for the team, expenses for individual training, and the love and support that only a loved one could give. Having a quality coach will help the individual learn how their performance and skills fit into the team's big picture.

Sleeping enough is critical to having energy in practices and on game days, in addition to recovering from training. Appropriate soccer nutrition will increase the energy and endurance of a soccer player, help the soccer player achieve the ideal physique, and significantly aid in the recovery of the athlete. Understanding soccer positions more deeply than just knowing that there are forwards, midfielders, and defenders will help to determine if a certain type of role is better suited given your skills or if there is a player in a similar position as yours that you can look to guidance on effectively playing that position. Last, but not least, is developing a mindset that leaves you unshakable. This mindset will help you become knowledgeable on specific game situations, learn how to deal with other players, and be mentally tough enough to not worry about circumstances that you cannot control, such as the type of field you play on or the weather. The pyramid is a great visual aid to consider when choosing what areas to read next as a soccer player, coach, or parent. Now that you know where *Soccer Passing & Receiving* plays into the bigger picture, let us begin.

Chapter 1

Speed of Play

In soccer, how fast your team can move the ball impacts your team's effectiveness. Although you do not always need to play at a high speed of play, letting the ball do most of the work will help save your team's legs so that you will have the stamina needed during the last minutes of a close game. **Using the speed of the ball will surely provide openings that would otherwise be absent.**

Take for example the Spanish national team from 2008 to 2012 and the Barcelona club team during a similar period. Both teams used the passing technique of Tiki-Taka (one or two touch passing) to wear down opponents by passing the ball, so that the other side may go for a stretch of 10 or so minutes without even touching the ball. Forcing the other team to constantly play defense and chase the ball allowed the Spanish national team to win the Euro 2008, the 2010 World Cup and Euro 2012. Barcelona triumphed to the tune of six trophies in 2009 (Copa del Rey, League, Champions League, Spanish Super Cup, European Super Cup, Clubs World Cup). **The style of play involving considerable passing is excellent for reducing the hope of the other team when they barely have any time with**

the ball. In fact, in a study published by *The Telegraph* of the English Premier League from the 2009/2010-2013-2014 seasons, the team with more possession won roughly 50% more games than the team with less possession.

To be a capable passer desiring an increased speed of play, consider passing the ball into space. **Playing the ball into space helps teammates continue to run when they go to take their first touch on the ball**, which keeps your team's progress going towards the other teams net. Additionally, move the ball out of high-pressure areas on your third and the middle third of the field to decrease the number of unnecessary turnovers your team gives away.

Think faster, act faster. In order to think more quickly, look before you receive the ball so that you can develop a plan. Also, practice the skills you will use in a game, so they become second nature and need minimal thought. What separates good soccer players from the great soccer players is intelligence. Intelligence comes from experience. Therefore, one of the best ways to become better at soccer is to play it. However, keep in mind that it does not need to be your experience that provides you with the intelligence. **A wise person is one who can learn from others' mistakes and experiences.** Therefore, this book will help tremendously together with the constant desire to continue learning, which will help you grow into the soccer player you want to become. Learn from the soccer players you aspire to be like to reduce the time it takes to be the best on your team and in your league.

To improve your speed of play, always look to pass the ball into space to continue a teammate's momentum. Passing into space helps you dictate the play even when you no longer have the ball. Have a plan to act faster when you receive the ball. Furthermore, keep developing your knowledge of the sport to refine your skills and abilities continually. Remember that the topics discussed in this book are situational. Being able to make quality decisions is key and improving your knowledge of soccer is a quick way to decide on the best course of action during game situations.

Chapter 2

Passing with the Inside of Your Foot

As a soccer player, it is important to have the fundamentals down when it comes to passing. You can pass the ball with different parts of your foot, but the form that should be your most frequently used passing form is with the inside of your foot as follows:

1. Plant next to the ball while pointing your foot and hips at your teammate
2. Toe up, heel down, and ankle locked
3. Knees slightly bent and foot slightly off the ground
4. Follow through after making contact with the ball

1. The form for a pass and shot are different. **With passing form, you can (and should) plant much closer to the ball because your body mechanics allow you to turn your leg and pass the ball with the inside of your foot.** Similarly to a shot, you want to have the leg that is planting on the ground pointed at the person or the open space to which you are passing the ball. You have your plant leg slightly bent, which is the same for your shooting form. You definitely do not want a straight leg when you will plant for a shot or a pass. Also, turn your hips towards the person or area on the field that you are passing the ball.

2. **Point your toe all the way up, which makes your heel go down.** Having your toe up and heal down naturally locks your ankle. Having a locked ankle will make it so that you have a powerful and more accurate pass. Also, locking your ankle allows the surface of your foot that you are passing the ball with (the side of your foot) to be wider. A more narrow foot creates more room for error so that if you miscalculate a little bit where the ball will be, you have a broader surface to ensure a more accurate pass. Conversely, if your toe is pointed down and your heel is up, your ankle will be loose, resulting in a lack of power on your pass. Also, you are making your foot smaller and narrower, which means that your pass will be inaccurate if misjudged even slightly regarding where the ball will be.

3. **Have the knee from your passing leg slightly bent.** You do not want a straight leg when you are passing. In fact, you do not want straight legs in most instances in the game at all. When you straighten your leg and stand completely up, it makes it so that you are not engaging the strongest muscle group of your legs, which is the quadriceps. This reduces your ability to be explosive with your shooting, passing, dribbling, running, jumping... Having a bent leg naturally makes it so that your foot will be slightly off the ground. If you pass the ball with your foot touching the ground or close to the ground, the pass will result in the ball popping up in the air. Part of passing is to make sure that you are making it as easy as possible for your teammate. After all, soccer is a team sport, so if you are consistently passing the ball in the air, you are making it more difficult for your teammates. Your teammates will likely then have to focus their first touch on controlling the ball on the ground and then their second touch of the ball allows them to attack into space. Ideally, your pass should be firm, accurate, and on the ground so that their first touch can be into space on the field.

4. **Next, make sure you follow through on your pass.** What you do with your leg after you completely follow through depends on the situation that you are in during the

game, scrimmage, or practice. Most times, after you make a pass, you will be running to another spot on the field to keep developing the play. Therefore, as you pass the ball (similar to a shot), you follow through and land on your passing foot. Then, you bring your back leg forward to take the next step. As you pass, you are already starting to continue to run and maintain your forward motion to the next spot on the field that you want to go. However, at times you will be passing the ball, while not being a part of the attacking portion of that play. For example, players that may do this are a goalie or in a few instances, a defender. Therefore, you follow through after you pass the ball, but then you bring your leg back to where it began the passing motion. As a result, you end up in the same spot you started when you are making this pass.

Keeping your head down while you pass the ball keeps your chest over the ball and holds your form together for a more accurate pass. Having your head over the ball reduces the chance that the ball will pop up into the air when you pass the ball. As you may have noticed, this is an excerpt from the first book in the series, *Soccer Training*. This chapter is entirely related to passing and receiving, so this was included to make sure that you were able to read this high-quality information in both books.

Chapter 3

The Weight of Your Passes

To ensure the ball gets to your teammate and they can expect to have a reasonable first touch, a soccer player must consider the weight of their passes. More specifically, the weight of a pass is how hard or soft the person making the pass plays the ball. How hard you pass the ball has a significant impact on whether your pass is intercepted, travels to your teammate, or your teammate does not have enough time to react to receive the ball. Some of the considerations when passing are:

1. How far away is your teammate?
2. How much pressure is your teammate under?
3. How good at receiving passes is your teammate?

1. **The distance between you and your partner is key in the power you have on your pass.** If your partner is only 5-7 yards from you, then you do not need to be concerned with having a powerful pass. In these instances, it is more important that you pass it to the correct foot or slightly in front of the correct foot, given the game situation. However, if your teammate is 20+ yards from you, softer passes will often be intercepted by a defender, so the pace of your pass

is critical. It needs to be powerful to ensure your team keeps possession.

2. **If your teammate has one or two defenders around them, then your passes need to be harder because of an increased chance of the opposition can interrupt the pass.** Though harder passes are often more difficult to handle at shorter ranges, it is the responsibility of the teammate to control it or you to find a better option for what to do with the ball. Remember to lead your teammate out of pressure with your passes. If they have a person on their backside and one to their right, play the ball to their left to make it easy for them to find more space than if you played it to their other side.

3. **Consider the receiving abilities of the person you are passing the ball.** The better they are, the harder you can pass the ball, as they will be more likely to receive the ball appropriately. If your teammate that you are passing the ball to is not as coordinated, then pass it slower, but if they are under pressure, then consider passing the ball to a different teammate altogether. Similarly, if you have better chemistry with this teammate, let this impact the weight of your pass as well. Also, consider if you are passing to their dominant or opposite foot. Remember, always assume a teammate or opponent is right-footed until they prove you otherwise.

Follow through on your passes to create greater accuracy and oftentimes, more power. Pass with the inside of your foot towards the heel for the hardest part of the inside of your foot to increase the weight of the pass. Furthermore, swinging your leg faster will generate more power on your passes too. Increase the pace of the pass when a teammate is further away, under pressure, and has good receiving skills. Pass it more softly when your teammate is closer, has little pressure, and is not good with their feet.

Chapter 4

Masking Your Passes with the Outside of your Foot and Toes

I n the second book of the Understand Soccer Series, *Soccer Shooting & Finishing: A Step-by-Step Guide on How to Score*, there is an entire chapter on shooting the ball with the outside of your foot and another chapter on shooting the ball with your toe. For this book, the form is very similar, but the application of when to pass with the outside or toes of your foot is slightly different. Passing with the outside of your foot or your toes helps to mask your passes, so the defense will not be thinking you are making a pass when you do. To start, an outside of the foot pass is extremely effective for the following reasons:

1. Deceptive to the other team's defenders, midfielders, and forwards when you will pass the ball.

2. A significant amount of curve to pass around players on the other team.

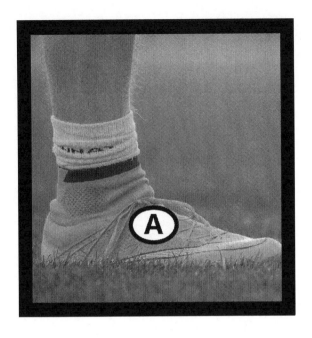

From this image, use the bone of your foot, which is point "A". Additionally, **point the toe of your passing foot down and in, so that you may you use this portion of the foot to pass.** An outside of the foot pass is one of the most deceptive passes in the game. You pass the ball with the same portion of your foot that you would use if you were to dribble the ball. Therefore, it does not look like you will pass the ball most times when you go to actually pass it. Having a pass that does not look like a pass is terrific because most soccer players that pass the ball with an inside of the foot pass will find that defenders are often able to jump in front of the pass to intercept the ball. Since players on the other team often slide or lunge to be in front of the ball when you are passing, pass fakes are often very useful. More often than not though, you will be passing and not doing a pass fake, which may result in the defender deflecting or fully stealing the ball when you attempt to pass it to a teammate. Often, this leads to a fast break for the other team.

Next, an outside of the foot pass is handy because it allows you to cause a curve in the path that the ball takes. The curve is similar to that of a bent pass but often with more power similar to a driven pass. A bending pass is tremendous because you can receive more passes that are not going to be blocked because the defender assumes you are still dribbling instead of passing.

The outside of the foot pass allows you to diversify the way you can pass the ball to a teammate to continually keep the other team's players guessing. **When a defender knows you can use any part of your foot or can use either one of your feet, they tend to give you more space.** When they give you more space, it makes it even easier for you to have time to shoot, pass, dribble, or do whatever you need to do on the field. The defender will give you a certain amount of space and respect making your passing and receiving a little bit easier as the game goes on. Also, because your outside of the foot pass is going to be a bit curved, this enables you to find a passing lane that may not have been there otherwise.

Outside of the foot passes are very threatening when you are attacking down the sideline and cross the ball into the box before the defender even realizes what you are doing. Keep in mind that you should only develop the outside of the foot pass once you have become very comfortable with an inside of the foot pass driven shot. Please note that passing with the outside of your foot involves you turning your toes down and in to hit the ball with the laces of your cleats, which is directly on top of the bone of your foot. Performed this way, it allows you to place the hardest part of your foot on the ball to increase the power on your pass. Consider looking at Ricardo Quaresma for a great example of a player who effectively uses the outside of his foot.

When you first start playing soccer, you instinctively start off kicking the ball with your toe. You are quickly told that using a toe poke/toe blow is incorrect and that you should be using the bone of your foot to pass. In fact, many of my trainees have made fun of other trainees when they kick the ball with their toe. The trainees have been so conditioned that using their toe is incorrect, that they are confident enough to tease others who use it. However, after playing soccer with that limiting belief for the last 15 years, I have come across three instances that have entirely shifted my mindset over the last few years on why **a toe poke shot or pass can be great**.

First, when in a scrimmage against another team, the other team's coach had stopped his player after an attempt to score. The coach pulled the player and told him "when you are that close to the net, do not be afraid to toe poke/toe blow the ball if that is the only way you can take a shot. A shot with your toe is going to be a lot better than no shot at all." For me, the other team's coach drove home the message that taking more shots is going to result in more goals, even if they are not perfect shots. The chance may end up being a lucky and accurate shot, the goalie may mishandle the ball resulting in a goal, or the goalie may give up an easy rebound for yourself or a teammate to shoot the ball into the back of the net.

Second, it was a handful of years ago during the "El Clásico" between the world's two largest soccer clubs: Barcelona and Real Madrid. The game ended in a draw because of Cristiano Ronaldo's goal. The average soccer fan watching simply saw that the ball went in the net. However, on closer inspection of the goal, a viewer could notice that the ball was played a little too far in front of Cristiano Ronaldo for him to shoot any other way than to use a toe poke/toe blow. This example points out that you can extend your leg further in front of you to reach the ball by using your toes to kick the ball, which means that you can reach further out and allow yourself to pass more over your career when you understand that using your toe to pass is acceptable.

Third, there was a light bulb turning on while watching a highlight reel of outstanding goals. The only goal that stood out was Ronaldinho's goal, which says a lot since the video was several minutes long. Ronaldinho's goal was when he was still playing for Barcelona. On the YouTube video highlight reel, he scored from just outside the 18-yard box. He was standing still for a few seconds looking for a pass. The defender gave him as much time as he wanted as the defender felt he had stopped Ronaldinho from advancing with the ball or being able to shoot. The defender was standing in front of Ronaldinho and was waiting for him to make a move when Ronaldinho decided to toe blow the ball, which resulted in him scoring a goal.

If you have watched any of Ronaldinho's highlight videos before, then you have likely seen this goal and can imagine it right now. A key takeaway from this is that using a toe poke/toe blow creates deception that allows you to make a pass off more efficiently. The defender was not expecting Ronaldinho's strike with his toes. The defender figured that it would be unrealistic for Ronaldinho to have any power on a shot given that he was standing still. The defender had it in his mind that he would either pass the ball or shoot a weak shot that the goalie could easily stop. However, Ronaldinho being the cheeky player that he is, thought of a fancy and effective way to make the best out of the possible options he had available. He sought an opportunity to improve his team's chances of winning by toe poking/toe blowing the ball and took complete advantage of it. He was close enough to the net (on the 18-yard box) to have a toe blow as a viable option. If he were any further from the net, it would not have been reasonable to use his toe to strike the ball.

Therefore, by using the toe of your foot during appropriate game situations, it allows for three things that using the inside of your foot often does not:

1. Provides an additional way for you to make a pass. Make sure to strike the ball just below the center of the middle of the ball when doing a toe poke/toe blow.

2. Allows you to extend your leg so that you can make more passes by being able to reach further.

3. It is very deceptive to use a toe blow because most soccer players do not think that people will use their toe to kick a soccer ball, so it is misleading. You do not have to extend at the hip (only at the knee) as you would with the form for an inside of the foot pass, so it takes less time to make a pass, which makes it very easy to disguise the pass.

One common trap that players fall into when it comes to passing with the outside of their foot is that they master passing with only their dominant foot and do not develop their opposite foot. The soccer player can compensate by just passing with the outside of their dominant foot instead of developing their opposite foot. An example of a player that relies exclusively on his dominant foot is Mesut Ozil. He spends energy and time avoiding his opposite foot that could be used to help his team score. Sadly, he is likely afraid to work on it for fear of failing, which is all too common with many soccer players. You probably will not make it as far as you want in your soccer career if you cannot use both of your feet. The number of opportunities in a game that exists for you to use your opposite foot is tremendous and for you to go your entire career without using both feet is very detrimental for your confidence too.

Next, another outstanding way to mask your pass is to point towards an area of the field that you do not intend on passing towards. 9 times out of 10, the defender will take one or two steps towards that direction (the wrong direction) which gives you space in the direction that you either want to attack towards or make a pass. Pointing is an advanced technique that takes no soccer skill on the ball, just a good sense of when to use it.

In conclusion, passing with the outside of your foot and your toes allows you to be deceptive to defenders and the goalkeeper. The outside of your foot allows you to bend the ball when you pass. Additionally, a toe blow pass is quicker than an inside of the foot pass, making a pass with your toe great to use after a shot fake or pass fake to ensure you can pass the ball past the defender. Master the inside of the foot pass before you spend a considerable amount of time on the outside of the foot pass or toe poke pass. It is an intermediate to an advanced level style of passing that can be made even better when you point in a different direction than you intend to pass.

Chapter 5

Effective Crossing

Effectively being able to cross the ball means that you can place in it in the area where a teammate can easily and efficiently take a shot or have a header on net. Not only do you have to worry about making it easy for a teammate but you also have to make it as difficult as possible for the other team's defenders and goalie from intercepting, deflecting, or clearing your cross.

To start, when making a cross from the wing, **often the best area to cross the ball into often is the "danger" area**. The danger area between the 6-yard box and the penalty spot. A cross into the danger area is often too far in front of the goalie for him or her to react quickly enough to grab the ball. This area is often behind the "backline" (the line across the field the defenders make), which places a defender in a compromised and risky position of having their body facing the net when attempting to clear a cross. The 2018 World Cup saw the most own goals ever scored in a World Cup because the players crossing the ball were so precise at delivering the ball into the danger zone. Keep in mind that the positioning of players is always changing.

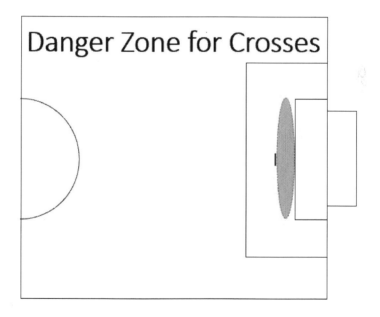

Danger Zone for Crosses

Therefore, the situation changes resulting in a need to revise your plan to score. However, a cross into the danger zone is often a much higher probability cross than other crosses. Make sure your teammates know this is where most your crosses will be, so they will give the effort to ensure they are in front of the net to score. One player that does a fantastic job of crossing the ball consistently into the danger zone is Kevin De Bruyne who plays for Manchester City and the Belgium National Team. Time after time he is making crosses into this area on the field, which often explains why he is one of the top assisters if not the top assister each season in the league.

Next, driven crosses (fast crosses) leave the goalie less time to react but leaves less time for a teammate to respond too. Generally, when you play a driven ball into the box, you want to play it no higher than waist level because it will be going too fast for a teammate to head the ball consistently. Additionally, driving it closer to the ground increases the chances that even if it is not an accurate pass, it may take a deflection and settle perfectly for a teammate to score.

Another cross to consider is the bent/curved cross. **Bent/curved crosses make it harder for the goalie to judge where the ball will be**, but it also makes it harder for a teammate to decide where the ball will be as well. A bet/curved cross will likely need to be lofted and is a great cross for teammates to score off of a header.

Keep the ball on the ground if your teammate that you are crossing to has no defenders in front of him or her. Otherwise, loft the ball so they can shoot it or head it in. Why cross the ball, which forces your teammate to consider trapping the ball, before being able to shoot or pass? You can just as easily play them a pass that allows them to strike a one-time shot or take a useful attacking touch to help your team score.

Avoid switching the field in the air if that teammate has a defender on them. Unless you are under intense pressure, crossing the ball to a teammate with a defender on them will decrease the odds that your team maintains possession of the ball. Your team goes from you having 100% possession of the ball to you giving your teammate a 50-50 chance at winning the ball. Instead, consider looking for a closer teammate, so that you can make an accurate pass on the ground.

Try to avoid doing cross fakes when driving down one of the wings. Though it may work to fake out your defender, it will also fake out your teammates and result in them having poorly timed runs that can be easily countered by the other team. For example, you are dribbling with quick speed down the sideline and you have a defender in a foot race with you. You have teammates crashing the net expecting you to cross the ball when you pull your leg back, so they ensure that they are in what they believe are high probability spots for you to cross the ball. Just then, you decide to do a cross fake and all of your teammates are now correctly positioned if there were an actual cross, but too early given that you have not crossed the ball yet. After your cross fake, you immediately cross the ball, but your teammates have been standing in the correct position for a few seconds, which allowed the defenders the time to properly cover your teammates. Now, your teammates have a much lower chance of being able to do anything with the ball and an increased chance of being offside.

Furthermore, it is often better to not even cross the ball if it is obvious that the other team's goalie will intercept the ball and if your entire team is on the opposition's half of the field. **Crossing the ball in this situation where the chances are great that the goalie will catch the ball, you are giving him or her a freebie to start a counterattack against your team quickly.**

In conclusion, be thoughtful when crossing. Understand that the danger zone is ideal for crosses, driven crosses need to be waist-level or lower, and bent crosses are ideal for a teammate to head the ball. When you want to cross the ball ultimately, avoid cross fakes, but know they are beneficial if your desire is to continue to dribble with the ball and not actually cross it.

Chapter 6

Should You Heel Pass?

Given that this book is about passing and receiving, one of the more common passing forms players use is attempting to pass the ball with their heel. A heel pass, when completed, can look wonderful. It is similar to that of an upper 90 shot. They both are low probability, but when they work, they look spectacular. **With that being said, heel passes have a low rate of success given that you are striking it with your heel.**

Furthermore, you are passing in a direction that you are no longer looking towards. Let us not forget that there is an excellent chance that the ball will not be lined up perfectly towards your teammate's direction, which would result in it being easily intercepted by the defender. Also, for you to make a heel pass, you need to go from dribbling the ball while being behind the ball, to swinging your foot all the way in the front of the ball. Then, pulling your leg back, you can finally strike the ball with your heel. Heel passes take a considerable amount of time and it is effortless for the defender to notice what you are doing and to step in front of the pass to intercept it. An intercepted pass in this scenario where you are going one way and passing it in the complete opposite direction will often result in the other team having a quick counter-attack.

One famous soccer player that has used the heel pass on several occasions and has made himself look quite ridiculous in the process is the forward Mario Balotelli. Given that he is quite the showman, he likes to perform the low probability of success skills that look cool when completed. The problem often is that because he performs skills that are unlikely to work, when he does not complete one of them, he looks foolish.

He played in a game at the Herbalife World Football Challenge. He was in front of the net playing with Manchester City against LA Galaxy. He decided against making an easy pass to a teammate or even shooting the ball himself only 15 or so yards from the net. In fact, there was not a single defender in front of him or his teammate. He decided to fully rotate his body so that his back was facing the ball in order to strike the ball with his heel. He missed the net quite significantly. The entire fan base was in disbelief as well as the coach, who immediately substituted him out. Similarly, his teammates questioned his ability to make decisions and this was one of the many scenarios that led to his ultimate downfall from the heights that he had achieved in soccer.

In conclusion, heel passes are not that effective because they take too long to strike the ball with your heel. To successfully complete a heel pass, you have to bring your leg fully in front of the ball, which is very obvious to the defender and often makes it easy for them to cut off the pass. Please understand that this is not to say that a heel pass should never be used, because there are those rare occasions when the ball rolls behind you and there is a clear passing lane to a teammate, but it should be used infrequently. Hitting the ball with your heel results in passes that are not likely to be accurate. You will notice that passes with your heel generally gives possession of the ball to the other team or places your teammate receiving the pass in a 50-50 situation. Neither are good when you are aiming to be an effective passer.

Chapter 7

Receiving the Ball

You can receive the ball with different parts of your foot, but the five general rules to receive a pass, listed in chronological order to ensure ball control and an accurate first touch are:

1. Plant next to the ball while pointing your foot and hips at your teammate
2. Toe up, heel down, and ankle locked
3. Knees slightly bent
4. Foot slightly off the ground
5. Typically, use the inside of the foot towards the heel to take an attacking touch

The form to receive a pass is the same as the first four steps of the form to make a pass. However, to receive a pass, there are a few more things to consider to make sure that you are productive with the ball:

1. **Demand the ball; do not ask for the ball. Yell for the ball; do not call for the ball.** These shifts in wording (demand versus ask and yell versus call) do a few excellent things for you as the person that wants to receive a pass or

be played a through ball. A through ball is when someone plays the ball in front of you and into space allowing you to run to the ball and continue your forward momentum at full speed.

Demanding the ball lets the person that is passing the ball know that you are very confident. It tells him or her that you will do something with the ball that is beneficial for your team. Think about it, if you are playing a game and have two people that you can pass the ball. The first person is screaming their head off demanding the ball. The other person is maybe showing for a pass, using a hand motion indicating that they want the ball, or meekly asking for the ball. Even if the person that is yelling for the ball is not quite as open, the player with the ball will consider passing it to them because they can hear it in their voice that they plan to do something with the ball. Also, demanding/yelling for the ball even if the person with the ball is close to you, ensures that he or she hears you.

Often, the person dribbling the ball is far away from you or potentially has a defender or two covering them. Therefore, by demanding/yelling for the ball, you let them know that you are open to receive the ball. **Many available passes in soccer are not made because the player with the ball did not know you were open.** They have their head down and looking at the ball, to protect the ball from the defender. Therefore, if they do not hear you with their ears, they are likely not going to see you with their eyes. Lastly, yelling for the ball builds confidence in yourself and increases your ability to help your team achieve its offensive objective of scoring!

2. **Depending on the situation in the game, you want to make sure that you check to the ball (go towards the ball) in most instances.** Now, you definitely do not want to do that when you are making a "through" run and you want them to play the pass in front of you. In these situations, you want to communicate (yell/hand motion/or start sprinting in a direction away from the play, but down the field) to them where you are going and let them pass the ball in front of you so that you can take your first touch in stride. More often than not, you will be receiving a pass and you should be checking to the ball to make sure that you successfully receive the ball.

One of the more frustrating things for a coach and a teammate is when you are passed a good (not a great) pass and you are not able to receive the ball because you are playing lazily. You must be active, on your toes, and going to receive the pass. If you do not, it allows the defender to come between you and the ball. This laziness results in an intercepted pass, which makes it very easy for the other team to have a counterattack due to you losing possession during a simple pass.

3. **Before receiving a pass, make sure to scan the field and look behind you.** Having a good idea of what you plan to do before you actually do it will make you a much more effective and efficient soccer player, as well as a better teammate. It does not have to be a 5 to 10-second scan. It is just a quick swivel of the head to see if there is pressure and where some open teammates are for you to make a sensible pass or potentially dribble after you receive the ball. A quick look is something that sets college players apart from high school players and definitely professional players from college players.

These differences are things that coaches and scouts notice. An excellent defender, midfielder, or striker will assuredly know where teammates and opponents are on the field. Therefore, as they are receiving the pass, they are already thinking about what their next actions in the game will be. In soccer and life, if you fail to plan, you plan to fail. **By quickly scanning behind you, you are already starting to allow yourself mentally to have time to develop a plan of attack.** The fast scan will surely help you score more or deliver the pass that will allow your team to score.

4. **Next, when you receive a pass in most game situations, you still want your hips to be square with your teammate.** Though when you are along a sideline this advice may change, being squared with your teammate means that you are pointing your hips at your teammate. When your hips are square with your teammate, you will be more accurate with your first touch than if your hips are not pointing at your teammate. In this instance, you are creating an L with your stance by pointing your plant foot at your teammate. The foot you are receiving the pass with is turned, so that you can use the inside of your foot to take your first touch. This form is basically the same as if you were making a pass.

5. **Roughly 95% of your first touches in a game should be attacking touches.** An attacking touch pushes the ball into space with your first touch. An attacking touch is the opposite of taking a touch where the ball stops underneath you (at your feet). An attacking touch may go towards your opponents net, towards your own net, or in any direction away from where you are currently. In a game, you should mostly be taking attacking touches because it allows you,

with your first touch, to already have the ball going in the direction that you want to take it.

More often than not, the first attacking touch is into space on the field to give yourself more time to think, to pass, to dribble, to shoot, to do whatever you need to do with the ball. Next, by taking the first step with your attacking touch, you will have a more accurate first touch. Looking at the picture, use part "B" to take an attacking touch with the hardest part of your foot, which can be referred to as the "bat."

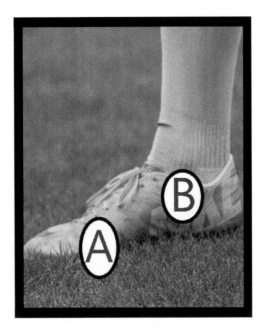

Your attacking touch is not meant to push the ball really far away from you; it is intended for you to take your first step in the direction that you want to go. **An attacking touch was something I did not realize for the longest time that was key to being a fast soccer player.** I thought that you had to be a quick runner to be a fast soccer player. In reality, you have to be great with your first attacking touch to be a fast soccer player. This one tip alone changed my game overnight. The attacking touch helps your acceleration tremendously because you are already starting to build momentum and speed in the direction that you want to go, which enables you to distance yourself from the defender that is marking you.

6. **Occasionally, it will be appropriate to take a touch underneath your body (a touch that stops at your feet).** This touch is necessary when you have too many people around you where someone could easily cut an attacking touch off and take possession of the ball from you. Only then is it okay to take your first touch under your body. Also, if you receive a difficult pass, ideally you still take an attacking first touch, but it is understandable if you take a first touch that stops underneath you and then you start attacking with the ball. Bad passes are generally ones played to you in the air. Looking at the picture again, use part "A" to take a touch with the softest portion of your foot, which can be referred to as the "broom" to settle the ball at your feet.

7. When you move to receive the pass, what you plan to do with the ball determines which portion of your foot to use to take an attacking touch. **Ideally, the attacking touch is really going to be an attacking step.** You are pushing the ball with the same portion of your foot (the inside of your ankle) that you pass a ball with because it should be locked and will push the ball better. However, if you are looking for the ball to stop underneath you, you will be taking your first touch with the inside of your foot up towards your toes.

There is space in your shoe between your toes, there is a lot more fabric, and a lot less bone towards your toes. This area of your foot is your "broom" and because your "broom" is not very hard, the ball will stop underneath you. Look at the portion of the foot labeled "A" in the previous image. Additionally, if you are looking to have your first touch go completely behind you so that you can continue to accelerate away from pressure and into space, then you can take the touch even more softly towards the inside of your foot using your toes (using the "broom"). Do this more softly than if you wanted to stop the ball underneath you. This much softer touch is so that the ball does not go racing by you. You can slow it down a little bit, but not stop it entirely because you want to be attacking in the space directly behind you.

Chapter 8

Receiving with the Correct Foot

To be a productive player on the field, you want to make soccer as easy as possible for you and as hard as possible for the opposing team. One way to ensure that you are increasing the chances of your success is to receive the ball with the correct foot. Now, understand that this advice is not for 100% of circumstances, but can be used in many game situations, so that you can quickly fire a shot, play a pass, or dribble the defender.

To start, you generally want to receive with the foot that is in the direction that you want to go. Specifically, if you are looking to attack to the left, receive the ball with your left. If you are going to the right, then take your first touch of the ball with your right foot. Doing this allows your first touch to be a first step in the direction that you are looking to go, enabling you to already start generating some momentum. On the contrary, if you wanted to attack to your left, but took your first touch with your right foot, you would naturally have to cross your feet. Crossing your feet is generally regarded as unathletic. Furthermore, your touch will often be less accurate because you will often turn your hips too much when crossing your feet. So instead of a consistent touch in the direction that you want to go, you will have crossed feet and semi-accurate first touches.

Next, the general rule mentioned in the previous paragraph applies when you have your back facing the net you need to score in as well. **However, when attacking forward, you want to use the inside of your foot and when you want to attack behind you, use the outside of your foot to push the ball.** When taking that attacking first touch, make it the first step too. As mentioned previously, it already generates momentum in the direction you plan to go. It also increases your accuracy by your step naturally creating a follow through to ensure the ball goes in the direction you need it to go.

Remember, this is not advice for every situation, but is applicable for roughly 90% of the time. There may be situations where you are a forward with a defender on your backside that has been preventing you from turning the entire game or a midfielder that is in an extremely crowded area of the field where it may become more appropriate to receive the ball differently. However, crossed legs create less than accurate touches and are not often risks to take when playing.

When receiving the ball, using the correct foot will add speed to your game to create time and space for you. When you need a touch that is several yards away, take the touch towards the heel on the inside of your foot, as this is a harder portion of your foot and will make the ball travel further. If you are in a high-pressure area with seemingly countless players on the other team surrounding you, then a touch with the inside of your foot towards the toes is ideal to settle the ball close to you, since the toes are the softer portion of your foot. Use the correct portion of your foot and the correct foot given the situation to become the great soccer player you want to be!

Chapter 9

Know Before You Receive the Pass

Soccer players generally reside in one of two groups. The first is that they react to what is happening to them on the field. The second group is made up of those who plan and act on that plan. The first type of player is often the one that only scores a couple of goals a season and they are also the player that is often lacking confidence on the field. The second type of soccer player is the person that leads the team in goals or assists, is looked at by their teammates for direction, and often plays every single minute of the entire game. Let us dive into what it takes to be a proactive player instead of a reactive player:

1. Take a quick look
2. Make a plan
3. Revise the plan as needed

1. Take a quick look over your shoulder when you are receiving the ball with your back facing the net you need to score in. **Looking up quickly before you receive a pass makes it easy to form a picture in your mind of where nearly everyone is on the field.** This image of the placement of teammates and opposition allows you to

decide on your plan of action, even while you are not looking at where you plan to go. Watch the professionals play to notice that a quarter of a second look, will dramatically improve their performance. Additionally, looking at the field before you receive the ball provides confidence on the ball because you know how heavily the other team is currently pressuring you.

2. **Make a plan of how to proceed once you receive the ball.** More often than not, you will not be passed the ball, so you will have to be continually revising your plan as you await a pass. Your positioning, the defense's form, and the person attempting to pass you the ball changes, so you need to adapt quickly. Now, you do not need a detailed plan for every dribble you take, but you do want a general idea of what you plan to do.

For example, you are standing in the middle of the field as a midfielder and you turn your head just before receiving the ball. You realize that there is pressure behind you to your right, but space to your left. Therefore, as the pass is played to you, you should take a step towards the ball so the defender does not intercept it. With your first touch, you guide the ball behind you to your left. It is as simple as that! Once you guide the ball there, then you take a quick look up and see if anyone is making a quality run, or if there is a forward checking to the ball that is open. Again, it is very simple. You made two plans in virtually no time. **Remember, these plans do not have to be rocket science, just you knowing what your next one or two moves are before you do them makes you much more effective.**

Another situation to mention is if you are a forward receiving a pass from a midfielder, you turn to look as you are checking to the midfielder, which allows you to realize that an outside midfielder is starting to make a run down the side of the field where there is a ton of space. Since you see they are creating a great opportunity, instead of trying to turn with the ball, you can play a one-time pass. One more instance is if you are an outside defender receiving a pass from your goalkeeper. As he or she is passing you the ball and you are checking to it, you take a quick look up the field to see a forward from the other team sprinting towards you. Excitingly, you one-touch it back to the keeper so they can go either up the field or to the other outside back with a pass. Seriously, all it needs to be is a one or two-step plan when you receive the ball.

The reason why coming up with a plan is essential is because visualizing your passes, foot skills, shots,... is nearly as effective as having practiced them

once before. Therefore, by creating a quick plan, it is roughly the equivalent of already having done what you are about to do. This visualization is key for acting upon others instead of reacting to others. Acting versus reacting is the difference between a team leader and a bench warmer.

3. Ideally, when you make a plan, everything will work exactly as you imagined it. However, this is hardly ever the case, which is why it is so **important that you can revise your plans quickly as you see different situations develop on the field.** Generally, you know how other players on your team and the other team will react, but more often than we would like, they do not do as we expected. If you read and learn more about what players are supposed to be doing and they do something different, this allows you to take advantage of the situation.

In conclusion, take a look to see what options are available. Then, make a short plan for what your intentions are. Afterward, keep following the plan until your assumptions change and you need to create a new plan or you have passed the ball to a teammate. At this point, make another plan. Do not overthink the plans, just keep a few key points in mind such as attack into space when receiving a pass, yell for the ball when you are open, and look for high probability passes to ensure that you are a terrific passer on your team.

Chapter 10

Find a Passing Lane

Something that players and coaches cannot stand someone that expects perfect passes over or under the opposition. It is your personal responsibility to get open for them to pass the ball directly to you with ease. Now this is not to say a difficult pass should never be made. However, roughly 90% of your passes should be ones that you are very confident will make it to a teammate. (Obviously, if the time is running out towards the end of the game and your team is losing or if your team is winning by a large margin, then you should consider more difficult passes if your options are limited).

If you do not initially receive the pass from your teammate, then KEEP MOVING to move into a better position for them to pass you the ball. It is likely that from their point of view you are not in an excellent position to receive the pass or you have not opened your mouth to let your teammate know you are open. One incorrect belief that plagued me during my youth was that I should not call for the ball. I thought that my teammate should dribble with his head up so that they could see me if I was open because if I called for the ball, the other team would know I was open.

The problem with the mindset of not calling for the ball was that my teammates often dribbled with their head down, which meant the ball was rarely passed to me. My incorrect mindset meant very few goals and very few assists a season for me because this limiting belief reduced the number of times I touched the ball. Additionally, calling for the ball will often draw a defender towards you, which can reduce the amount of pressure your teammate has. Therefore, be both assertive and a great team player at the same time. "Assertive" in a sense that you want the ball, while drawing pressure to create space to help decrease the number of the other team's players closing in on your teammate.

One favorable way to ensure that you can find a quality passing lane is to be deceptive with your runs. **A deceptive run is one in which you take two or three steps in a direction you are not planning on traveling and then exploding in a different direction.** A deceptive run is extremely beneficial because it can help create space that would have otherwise not been there. Furthermore, if you start a deceptive run going to the left, this will often require the defender to follow you. The exciting thing is that you know your intentions of a sneaky run, but he or she does not. Therefore, with your first two or three steps towards the left, they will start covering you, requiring them to begin to run to your left too. This means their momentum will be carrying them the wrong way when you decide to change your direction. In the first book in the Understand Soccer Series, *Soccer Training*, we discussed how hard and time consuming it is for a defender to go from running in one direction, stopping their bodies, and then going in another direction.

One standout player that comes to mind when talking about making quality runs is Cristiano Ronaldo. He can consistently score the tap in goals and headers that most other players cannot because he knows how to make a quality run. His pace and height surely help too but would be nothing if he did not know where to go to increase his chances of receiving the ball in front of the net.

In summary, be a player that does not expect perfect passes through the reaching legs of three defenders. Know that a spectacular ball in the air that is hard enough to prevent a player on the other team from intercepting the ball, soft enough for you to take a comfortable first touch, and in the perfect spot based on your run is more often than not an unreasonable request. Find passing lanes that are more reasonable to pass in and can ensure your team maintains possession to keep you on the offensive. The positive with remaining on the attack is that most players find they use more energy running after a ball the other team is passing than having possession themselves. Wear the other team out with runs into passing lanes that were made available from deceptive starts and demand the ball from your teammate to help relieve some of their pressure and increase your chances of receiving the ball.

Chapter 11

Tell Your Teammate Where You Want the Ball

Do not expect the pass that you want if you are unable to tell the person passing the ball exactly where you want it. **Point with your hands.** A suggestion is to open your hand in front of you if you want the ball at your feet, open your hand to the right if you want it slightly in front of you to your right, or open your hand to the left if you want it slightly in front of you to the left. Point to the spot on the field if you want the ball played well in front of you, so that you may sprint to the ball.

Make sure you communicate these hand signals to teammates to make this process easier and so they know what you want in a pass. Expressing where you want the ball is one of those skills that take no soccer abilities with the ball whatsoever. **Think about it, if there are several things that you can do to increase your ability to receive a good pass, most of which are things that are just as easy for you to do as they are for you not to do, you definitely should.**

Showing a teammate where you want the ball is most easily done during throw-ins, set pieces, and goal kicks. Point to where you want the ball, but point using your hand in a way that allows your teammate to see where you want the ball, but the person covering you cannot. For example, if you have a defender behind you, point using your thumb, but position your hand in front of you, so the defender cannot see where you want your teammate to pass the ball. Keep in mind that if you are doing this, there likely is not enough time for a fellow midfielder or forward to fully look where you are pointing your thumb, so this is often better reserved for when you are a forward or midfielder asking for the ball from a defender who has minimal pressure on him or her.

Therefore, let your teammate know you want the ball by demanding it (not asking for it) and yelling for it (not calling for it). Yell for the ball when you think you have a better chance of keeping possession or attacking. Use your hands to help you and your teammate be on the same page, which increases the chance that there is a successful pass. Keep in mind that the reverse works too. If you are the one with the ball, do not be afraid to point where you want your players to be either to ensure you will pass it to them or to create space for you to pass the ball to someone else.

Chapter 12

Receiving the Ball Out of the Air

deally, when passes are played to you, they are on the ground. However, this is not true all of the time. Occasionally, you are played a pass out of the air. **Taking a great touch out of the air depends on the pressure of the defense and how high the ball is played to you.**

If the ball is played to you in the air while you are under high pressure, then use the front of your shoulder or your forehead to take an attacking first touch in the direction you need to go. Obviously, this is easier said than done and takes practice to master. Using your forehead or shoulders is ideal to take the attacking touch of the ball out of the air.

When the ball is played in the air and you have time to control it, allow it to hit the ground just slightly before pushing the ball in a direction you want to go. Using the inside of the foot as an example, when the ball is passed to you in the air, judge where the ball will land. Once you can see roughly where it will hit the ground, position yourself at that spot. **Then, as the ball hits the ground and starts to bounce up into the air, position the inside of your foot just over the ball so that it bounces into your foot.** The ball bouncing into your foot will push it back towards the ground. Trapping the ball this way allows you to successfully trap the ball out of the air in a way that takes as few touches as possible and lets you continue attacking with speed.

Keep in mind that using the inside of your foot towards your toes will create a small touch because your toes are the softest portion of the inside of your foot. **For a touch out of the air that allows you to take a large attacking touch in the direction you want to dribble, then use the inside of your foot towards your heal.** This portion of your foot is harder and will make for a touch that travels significantly further.

Additionally, one mistake trainees often make is leaning back when taking a touch from a pass in the air after the ball just hit the ground. Tilting back changes the angle of your foot making it very easy for the ball to go right, left, upwards, or forward. Obviously, you want more certainty in your touch and the direction the ball travels. Therefore, have your body, shoulders, and chest over the ball, so even if your touch is not perfect, it will remain in front of you. As previously mentioned, if you mistakenly lean back, then it makes it easy for your first touch to be into the air and it could go left, straight in front of you, right, or even up and over you.

In conclusion, take your first touch on the ball when played to you in the air with either your forehead or shoulder when under significant pressure. When you have a bit more space, let the ball hit the ground and right as it starts to bounce up, have the inside of your foot there to push it back towards the ground. Keep your shoulders over the ball while doing this to increase the accuracy of your first touch. Leaning back shows you are a bit scared to receive the ball and will create a first touch that could end up going in many directions. Let us not forget that leaning backwards can leave you unbalanced when looking to take your next touch or step.

Chapter 13

Turning with a Defender on Your Back

As a soccer player that is looking to receive passes, you will often find yourself with your back turned towards the very thing you are aiming to score in, the other team's net. **It is incredibly important that you are able to effectively receive a pass, turn your body, and explode up the field.** Ideally, you should be able to do this all in one motion. Recently, this topic was the main focus of a training session for one of my trainees, Kylie Kade, who has aspirations of playing for the United States Women's National Team. Steps to consider when turning with a defender on your backside are:

1. Look over your shoulder before you receive the pass to feel comfortable demanding the ball if you have space and believe you can do something productive for your team. (Have your head on a swivel.)

2. Use your arm to help you balance and prevent the opposing team's defender from going around you to cut off the pass.

3. Either have your shoulders pointed directly at the ball when it is coming towards you (so that you are not showing which way you are going) or be tricky by using your body to fake like you are going one way when you are planning to push the ball in the other direction.

4. Use the outside of your foot to push the ball. It is not a first touch you are looking to take but a first step that includes the first touch, so that you can accelerate away more quickly from the defender.

First, it cannot be stressed enough that you should look behind your shoulder when you are preparing to receive a pass. Depending on the situation, it may be best to just hold the ball and wait for support. A quick look will allow you to know where you should push the ball or even if you should request a pass at all from a teammate. **Do not twist at the hips to look behind you because this takes too much time.** Only turn your head by using your neck to make sure that you can take a swift look at the field and the players behind you. If you do this and determine that you have space to attack then yell for the ball and demand that it be passed to you.

Second, as a soccer player, you will very rarely be called for having your hands on an opponent. As such, when you are ready to receive the pass with your back facing the net you are looking to score in, **keep your arm up for balance, but especially to hold back the defender to ensure you are the one to receive the pass and not the other team.** Having your arm up does not mean that you should hold onto them, but you should place your forearm against them to slow their attempt to travel around you to intercept the ball. Also, having your arm up allows you to feel where the defender is, which factors into your decision on how to turn.

Third, never show the defender where you are going by revealing it to him or her with your body. When turning with your back to the goal and a defender is on your backside, either have your shoulders pointed directly at the ball when it is coming towards you or be deceptive and use your body to fake like you are going one way when you are planning to push the ball in the other direction. **Having your body pointed directly at the ball does not reveal to the defender which way you are going**, which is good, but the defender will only commit to going in a direction that they believe you will be pushing the ball. This is why it is so effective to use your body to pretend like you are going one way, while your real intentions are to go the other way.

Therefore, have your shoulders turned slightly in the direction that you want your defender to think you are going. Many defenders read the opposing player's body language as much as they read where the ball is currently located when judging how to stop a player attacking with the ball. Therefore, if you show the defender the direction that you are not going, they will often overcommit to the wrong side. If the defender commits to the wrong side, it will make it very easy for you to dribble past the defender without worrying about slowing down the speed of play or having the defender steal the ball.

When taking a deceptive first touch, there are two options. First, if you are looking to take your first touch in the space to the area behind you to the right, then turn your body/shoulders slightly to the left (so the defender will assume you are going to the left) and raise your right leg so it looks like you will be pushing to the left. However, at the last second, before receiving the pass, move your right leg across your body so that you can push with the outside of your foot to go to the space behind you to the right. Do the opposite of this if you looking to go to the space behind you on the field, to the left. The second option for when you want to deceive a defender into thinking you are going to the area to the left behind you when you are really looking to go to the right is to start by pointing your body/shoulders slightly to the left, then look as if you will push the ball with your left foot.

However, pretend to push the ball with your left a bit too early, so that you can plant that left leg on the ground, and raise your right leg across your body to push the ball with the outside of your right foot. Think of this as a jab/feint where you miss receiving the ball with your left foot and take it with your right. You can choose which move suits you better. The first option takes some flexible ankles and the ability to pivot with the plant foot that is already on the ground. The second option provides for a very stable plant of the left foot just after you have purposely missed the ball to allow for quick acceleration out with your right foot. Therefore, the second option is my preferred option, but please try both and see which one feels better and is quicker for you.

Fourth, it is ideal to use the outside of your foot to push the ball when turning into the space diagonally behind you because it allows you to take your first touch/step without having your legs crossed when you plant to explode away. Crossing your legs is very unathletic and should be avoided when possible as it is hard to explode with speed and it is easier to become unbalanced. It is especially important to be active and on the toes/balls of your feet to be ready for any pass.

To take a smaller touch when turning with a defender on your backside, take your first touch/step with the outside of your foot toward your toes because this is a softer area on your foot and the ball will not bounce off as powerfully. For a bigger touch, use the portion of your outside foot towards your heels to push the ball since the ball will be pushed with the harder area of the outside of your foot. Push the ball far enough to create space between you and the defender.

Combine the four steps of check over your shoulder, lift your arm for balance and to prevent the defender from intercepting your pass, point your shoulders towards the person passing, and push the ball with the outside of your foot where the leather meets the laces. These steps will help you become a deceptive forward that is quickly able to make progress up the field, even if your back is turned to it. Turning with your back towards the net you need to score on is a skill that most soccer players never learn. However, if this skill is mastered, it will place you in an elite class of forwards that are confident and able to control the ball. Several players that are known for their ability to be a point man (a big presence capable of winning balls out of the air and connecting passes for smaller/quicker players) are

Karim Benzema, Edinson Cavani, Gonzalo Higuaín, Olivier Giroud, and Zlatan Ibrahimović.

Chapter 14

How to Shield the Ball

I t is crucial that you can protect the ball to ensure that you can distribute the ball to your teammates as necessary. To shield the ball appropriately, consider the following three things:

1. Have a low center of gravity
2. Spread your arms
3. Push the ball away from pressure

1. When shielding the ball when there is a player from the opposite team behind you, **it is vital that you have a lower center of gravity than the opponent that is reaching in for the ball.** A lower center of gravity will give you a solid foundation and base to make it nearly impossible for the other player to move you and take possession of the ball. Your center of gravity is how high your hips are from the ground, so within reason, bringing your hips down several inches or even a full foot will make it so that you are more stable and more difficult to push off the ball. This positioning is similar to that of a quarter squat where you squat 1/4th of the way down. This position is optimal to shield the ball from the other team.

2. **Have your arms out.** Having your arms out means both extending at the shoulder and at the elbow to make your body and your arms as wide as possible. Though you are often taught from a young age that you are not supposed to have your elbows or even your arms up, the referees will hardly ever call you for having your arm raised, especially when you are shielding the ball from a player on the other team. Having your arms out and using them as leverage to make it more difficult for the opposition to steal the ball increases the chance that you will effectively shield the ball and be able to pass it to a teammate. Having your arms out naturally makes you wider and therefore will take longer for

the defender to travel around your body and arms to steal the ball and even if this defender does, you would likely take a touch away from them to buy you more time. Use the area on your arm between your wrist and elbow to make contact and provide the best mechanical advantage while giving enough space between the ball and the defender.

3. When shielding a ball, it is crucial that you are not afraid to take a touch away from pressure. **A touch away from pressure will help generate some momentum, as well as make it so that you are buying more time to determine your decision on how you will pass the ball to a teammate.** If a player on the other team is coming to your right side behind you, then do not be afraid to push the ball more towards the left. Having the ball on the other side that the opposition allows you to keep your body entirely between the ball and the other team's player.

Obviously, your size and the size of your opponent makes a difference. If you are a 5'5" and you are going up against a 6'5," you will find that their leg length and natural strength will make it very difficult for you to shield the ball. **If you are at a significant size disadvantage, avoid situations where you may be required to shield the ball.**

In conclusion, keep your center of gravity low by going quarter of the way down into a squat. Spread your arms out at the shoulder and the elbow, so they are wide and away from you. Do not be afraid to move the ball away from pressure to ensure that you are able to shield the ball correctly. Watch Philipp Lahm, the German National Team star and Bayern Munich player, for a great example of a small player that follows the advice in this chapter to effectively shield the ball from his opponents.

Chapter 15

Examples of Corner Kick Set Plays

A corner kick is where someone on your team will need to pass the ball and hopefully someone on your side will be receiving the ball. As a result, let us discuss helpful positioning and a few set plays for corners to ensure your passing and receiving skills are on point.

In general, if you are a defender looking to score or produce an assist, position yourself towards the corner of the 18-yard box nearest the corner where the kick is being taken from. **Additionally, consider positioning yourself just outside the 18-yard box to shoot any clearance attempts by the other team.** This positioning helps for various reasons. First, it gives the person taking a corner kick a potential person to pass the ball. However, it is often recommended for the person taking the corner kick to cross the ball into the box because there is a high chance that a mistake by the defense or a deflection will allowf your team to have a close-range shot. However, if your team is severely disadvantaged when it comes to height, then consider passing it to the person at the corner of the 18-yard box and avoid crossing what would likely be a wasted cross.

Next, being the defender towards the corner of the 18-yard box nearest the corner kick is beneficial because more often than not, when a defender is clearing the ball, it will end up being cleared to this spot. Defenders do not often look behind themselves during a corner kick to be comfortable with heading the ball to the other side of the field from which the corner kick came. Also, the other team's defenders do not want to head the ball to the top of the 18-yard box, because they know a member of the other team will be standing there, waiting for a cleared ball to fire a shot at the net. Therefore, they can either clear it out on the goal-line, which gives your team another corner kick or towards the top corner of the 18-yard box, which is ideally where a defender on your team is placed.

When it comes to midfielders, if you are taller or have a good vertical leap, then definitely position yourself in the box to take a header off of a corner kick. However, keep in mind that you must row your arms back and extend your neck and head forward to hit the ball with your forehead to have the most powerful header possible. **Power is emphasized since headers are not scored often given they lack the needed speed to travel past the goalkeeper.** If you are shorter, then consider going toward the top of the 18-yard box in hopes that the ball comes out to you, so that you may strike it, or be towards the flag where the corner kick is not being taken in hopes of receiving a ball that sailed over nearly everyone's head. Keep in mind that as a midfielder, you have defensive responsibilities too, so unless you are really good at using headers, being in the 6-yard box will not be too advantageous.

Lastly, as a forward, your primary job is to score! Therefore, you better be in the box looking to get a head, knee, or foot on the ball. You have minimal defensive responsibilities, so feel free to screen the goalie to make it easier for your teammates to score and look for deflections and rebounds in front of the net.

A terrific corner kick play is one that is mentioned in the second book of the Understand Soccer Series: Soccer Shooting & Finishing. **This corner involves a quick restart where you grab the ball as quickly as it goes out, place it on the corner spot and have previously communicated to a teammate, so they make a run from the top of the 18-yard box to the near post to take a quick shot.** Even if they do not score from this angle, which they often will, there often is a rebound that another player on your team can shoot the ball into the back of the net. In fact, in a recent game, I was taking the corner kick. I sprinted to grab the ball, placed it on the corner spot and without even taking a step back, I played a pass on the ground towards the penalty spot. This corner is a pre-planned corner for me and another player on my team. He fired a successful shot towards the far post for a spectacular and much-needed goal to tie a team we were initially losing 3 to 0 against. Quick corner kicks often catch the other team off guard.

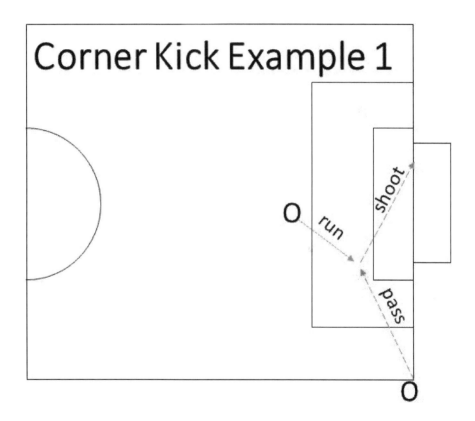

When you do not have any set plays established on your team, the ideal spot to place the ball is the penalty spot. The penalty spot is often further than the goalie is willing to travel, but still close enough to the net that there is a chance that you can score from a header. If the ball drops in that area, even better as it gives you a straight on shot to score.

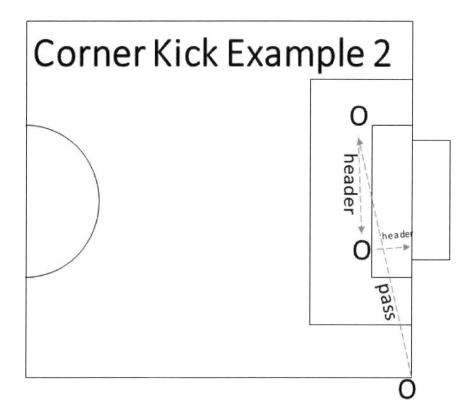

Finally, here are the details for a corner kick that takes a bit more coordination and is definitely an advanced level corner kick, as shown in the image. **Play a ball to a person on your team that is past the far side of the net.** That person then heads it to the post nearest where the corner kick was taken. Then, make sure this is communicated for a teammate to be there, but enjoy the outcome of this play, which is often a goal without a goalie directly in front of you. The initial cross nearly over everybody draws the goalkeeper to the post farthest from where the corner was taken. Therefore, when the ball is headed to the near post, the goalie will be stuck at the far post. The person at the near post will have an easier time scoring.

Even if the first header is not as accurate as the teammate receiving the pass needs, **the ball will still be in a dangerous spot in front of the net where the goalie is several steps away from.** When playing a corner into the 18-yard box, it is best to have a bent cross. Similarly to the fast restart, the bent shot/cross is discussed in the second book in the series, so check it out for the detailed steps on performing it. Bent crosses are so useful for corner kicks because they are difficult for the goalie to judge. Furthermore, they are lofted enough to travel over the other team's player that will likely be positioned as the first line of defense at the corner of the 6-yard box closest to where the corner is being taken. Conversely, you can take the corner kick short and have a person at the near post flick the ball to the far post.

In conclusion, the corner kick is a terrific chance for you to showcase either your passing or receiving skills.

Adjust where you are for the corner kick based on your size, abilities, and in what position you are playing on the field when you are not taking a corner kick. When you are the person taking a corner kick, either rely on a pre-planned corner or kick the ball towards the high probability area of the penalty spot.

Chapter 16

Examples of Throw-In Set Plays

Similarly to corner kicks, throw-ins offer a fantastic opportunity for you and a teammate to work on your passing and receiving skills. **To start, you likely know that you have to have both feet on the ground. You need to bring the ball back behind your head.** As you bring the ball forward, release it to pass the ball to a teammate. Therefore, let us dive into some of the unique things to consider when either taking a throw-in or being the person looking to receive a throw-in.

When you are the person taking a throw-in, you ideally want your throw-in to go towards a teammate's foot. This will allow them to take an attacking first touch immediately instead of having to settle the ball when it has been thrown to their chest or head. For example, when I was in high school, I considered a successful pass as one that traveled to my teammate. Not until late into my senior year of playing varsity soccer for one of the largest Division 1 schools in the state did a teammate tell me that I needed to keep my passes down.

He said that they were difficult to control and a pass in the air that could have just as easily been played on the ground should not be considered a successful pass. At first, due to a fixed mindset, I was a little bit offended that he was trying to correct the way I played. Then, after a considerable amount of time thinking about his comments, I realized that he was absolutely right and that a pass to a person's chest or head just was not good enough. As a result, I was able to better see when other teammates would make passes that looked similar to that and I now knew to avoid being a soccer player that set my teammates up for a greater chance of failure.

Too many of my teammates over the years had thrown the ball to my chest or head when there were only a few yards between us. Make it easy on your teammate if there is no defender between you and them. Have your throw-in travel towards their feet instead. This efficiently allows them to control the ball on the ground very quickly by taking an attacking touch with their first touch instead of worrying about needing to settle the ball. **If it takes two touches to go where you currently stand during a throw-in, to where you want to go, you likely will not have the luxury to take a second touch without it being met by a defender's foot attempting to poke the ball away.**

Next, as the person taking the throw-in, avoid playing to someone with multiple players covering them. Remember, a throw-in down the field may result in a turnover, but is often much safer than playing the ball back to a defender on your team who has a forward covering them. **Find the open** person, the person demanding the ball, or space on the field that a teammate starts to run towards.

Also, play the ball backward if your defender is open. Occasionally, you do not have time to go backward or you just do not trust your defender to do something productive with the ball. Avoid the defense in these situations, but **an open defender is often the easiest way to maintain possession on throw-ins.**

Additionally, an outstanding way for you, the person taking the throw-in, **to create space for your teammates is to fake one way, then throw the ball where you actually want it to go.** The other team will shift momentarily to cover where they initially believe you are throwing the ball, likely opening up space where you really plan to throw-in the ball. To do this effectively, do not scan the field by moving your head when you go to take a throw-in, but scan the field as you are going to collect the ball. When the ball is in your hands, point your hips in a direction you do not want the ball to go, then quickly adjust your foot stance to turn your hips to take a throw-in that catches the other team off guard.

More often than not, you will be the person looking to receive a throw-in than the person actually taking the throw-in. Something to consider when looking to increase your chances for a teammate to throw you the ball is to not immediately set up where you want the ball, **make a 2-3 step run in the wrong direction and then explode into**

open space that you just created to give your teammate an excellent option to pass you the ball. The person throwing in the ball will appreciate you making their job easier. Furthermore, your change of speed shows the person throwing the ball that you are very serious about receiving the pass.

Though significantly less frequent, walk over to your teammate as he is picking up the ball and **tell him exactly what you want to do**. This does not work as well when your team is behind because it takes time off the clock to communicate with them. At the very least, this will draw considerable pressure towards you because the opposition will think you will be the player receiving the ball. As a result, you will potentially create a situation where a teammate is poorly covered or open entirely. Taking pressure away from other players on your team may not be tracked directly on the stat sheet, but it will surely help your team score a few more goals over the course of a season.

In addition, **consider having a few set plays that your team organizes in a game**. First, have a set play where someone is 5 or so yards in front of the person taking the throw-in and have none of your teammates behind them. Then, as the throw-in is being taken have a person run in behind the person that is 5 yards away, so the teammate taking the throw-in may throw it further down the field. This play often creates a considerable amount of space behind the defense. Otherwise, another set play is a simple 1-2.

Start 5-7 yards away from the teammate taking the throw-in and by gesturing with your hands, show him or her a 1 and then a 2 using your fingers. This will indicate to him or her that you are preparing to pass the ball back with only one touch as soon as they play the ball to you. They will have a better vision of the field since they likely just scanned it to see who was open before they took the throw-in.

In conclusion, when you are the person taking the throw-in, play the ball to a teammate's foot when there are no defenders between you and them. Avoid high-pressure spots on the field when throwing the ball in. Consider playing the ball backward if you have an open and trustworthy defender. Also, consider using a fake to fool the other team. When you want the teammate taking the throw-in to pass you the ball, run into space so that you can more easily attack up the field. Potentially, walk over to your teammate and tell him or her exactly what you want to happen. Furthermore, have a set play or two for your team to increase the chances of not only maintaining possession of the ball during a throw-in but to quickly advance up the field on this set piece.

Chapter 17

One-Touch and Wall Passing

D o not be afraid of one-touch passing. Often players have one of two beliefs that reduce their desire to perform one-touch passing. First, if you pass the ball as soon as you receive it, you no longer have it to make an impact for your team. Obviously, this is far from the truth. A great soccer player looks for the best situations for their team to succeed, which will often be situations where the individual succeeds. Secondly, and much more common are **soccer players that are uncomfortable with using a one-touch pass because they are afraid they will mess up**. Sure, that may happen, but the best way to become better at something is to practice it. The same goes for one-touch passing.

Be sure to follow through with your passing leg to increase the accuracy. Consider passing 12 inches in the air for passes that are 7 yards or more to ensure that passes go over a defender's outstretched leg and so it has minimal friction by rolling on the ground. **One-touch passing speeds the pace of play up though, for many players, it can increase the chance of an inaccurate pass since you did not take a first touch to control the ball.**

Wall Pass (1-2 Pass)

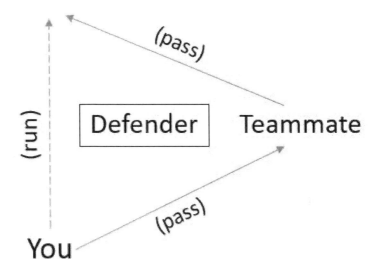

Therefore, consider a wall pass, which is also known as a 1-2 pass. **A wall pass is where you pass it to a teammate and they pass it back to you with one touch similar to if you were to pass a ball against a wall.** Wall passing helps to reduce your worry of not receiving the ball back. Additionally, wall passes are most often done when you are 5-10 yards from a teammate, which increases your chance for accuracy on your pass too! Avoid long distance wall passing as it increases your chances to mess up. Wall passing is best done around a defender. Allow the ball to do a significant amount of the work in place of you trying to use a foot skill to beat a defender. When possible keep your wall passes on the ground. Though some professionals can get away with wall passing the ball in the air, this again increases your chances for mistakes that lead to the other team stealing possession of the ball.

If you are the person starting the wall pass, you must explode after making your initial pass to your teammate. An explosive run indicates you want the ball back and will make it easier to create separation between you and the defender. However, wall passes can occur when neither you nor the person you pass the ball to move, but it will not help you move the ball around a defender this way. **Keep in mind that if your teammate makes several runs for you and you never reward them, do not expect them to keep making runs for you.**

An example of a player who is known for his passing, including his wall passing, is Xavi. Xavi was a player on the Spanish National Team with outstanding successes in 2008, 2010, and in 2012. Additionally, he was a player on the Barcelona team that won the 2014-2015 Champions League final. He was always looking for open space to travel into after his initial pass of the wall pass. He averaged 100 passes or so per game because of the effectiveness that passing around defenders brought to him and his team.

In summary, if you are the person starting a wall pass, you have to pass effectively and receive the pass efficiently. Perform wall passes when you are close to a teammate and use one-touch passing in a wall pass to make it quicker. One-touch passing is beneficial and can be significantly improved when practiced. To increase repetitions with it, try emphasizing it in practices, where mistakes are not as costly as they would be in a game. Also, by practicing using a wall, you will be working on your explosiveness and reflexes by being able to receive quick passes off the wall.

Conclusion

The main thing is to keep the main thing the main thing. This statement is so true in life and soccer. In soccer, the main thing to keep in mind is to develop the abilities that you are most likely to use on the field, without spending much time on those things that would be used only occasionally. Referring back to the preface of this book, the Individual's Pyramid of Importance concept is an excellent indicator for all of the topics in soccer to emphasize on what your practice time should be spent. For this book specifically, keep in mind that most of your time should be spent on the basic skills of passing with the inside of your foot, taking an attacking touch when receiving the ball, working on weighting your passes, and looking at pressure before you receive a pass.

This book and the other books in the series are meant to be read and understood, but also act as a guide to which you can refer back. Therefore, do not be afraid after you are done with this book to open it from time to time to get a refresher on the tips, tricks, tweaks, and techniques on improving your abilities. **Now, keep in mind that a soccer player that wants to take their game to the next level will do whatever it takes to find the information that will help take him or her there.** Then, he or she will implement the information in practice to ensure it can be used in a game. The process of reading about how to become better, focusing on improving in practice, and then playing better in a game provides for continued growth and progress in any soccer player's career. However, be skeptical about some of the people creating YouTube videos. Many of the "soccer experts" that I have recently found on YouTube are showing poor form. The poor form results from people with little experience actually using the skills themselves in a game. This book provides a great opportunity to read the words to gain the understandings needed to grow. Keep working to be the best player that you can be and I look forward to talking with you in the next book in the series.

If you enjoyed this book, please leave me a review on Amazon letting me know what you enjoyed.

Bonus!

Wouldn't it be nice to have the steps in this book on an easy 1-page printout for you to take to the field? Well, here is your chance!

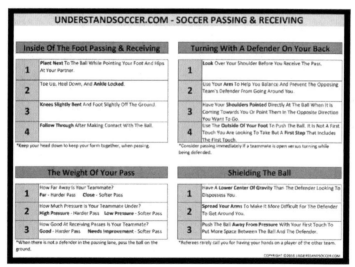

Go to this Link for an **Instant** 1-Page Printout:
UnderstandSoccer.com/free-printout

This FREE guide is simply a "Thank You" for purchasing this book. This 1-page printout will ensure that the knowledge you obtain from this book makes it to the field.

Free Book?

How would you like to obtain the next book in the series for free and have it before anyone else?

Join the Soccer Squad Book Team today and receive your next book (and potentially future books) for FREE.

Signing up is easy and does not cost anything.

Check out this website for more information:

understandsoccer.com/soccer-squad-book-team

Thank You for Reading!

Dear Reader,

I hope you enjoyed and learned from *Soccer Passing & Receiving: A Step-by-Step Guide on How to Work with Your Teammates*. I truly enjoyed writing these steps and tips to ensure you improve your game, your team's game, or your child's game.

While I was writing this book and having others critique it, I received some great insights on the book. As an author, I love feedback. Honestly, you are the reason that I wrote this book and plan to write more. Therefore, tell me what you liked, what you loved, what can be improved, and even what you hated. I'd love to hear from you. Visit UnderstandSoccer.com and scroll to the bottom of the homepage to leave me a message in the contact section or email me at Dylan@UnderstandSoccer.com.

Finally, I need to ask a favor. I'd love and truly appreciate a review of *Soccer Passing & Receiving*.

Reviews are a key part of the process to determine whether you, the reader, enjoyed my book. The reviews allow me to write more books and to continue to write articles on the UnderstandSoccer.com website. You have the power to help improve my book. Please take the 2 minutes needed to leave a review on Amazon.com at http://www.amazon.com/gp/product-review/B07CHYQTH8.

Thank you so much for reading *Soccer Passing & Receiving* and for spending time with me to help improve your game.

In gratitude,

Glossary

50-50 - When a ball is passed into pressure or cleared up the field and your teammate and a player on the opposing team each have an equal (50%) chance of taking possession of the soccer ball.

Attacking Touch - Pushing the ball into space with your first touch, which is the opposite of taking a touch where the ball stops underneath you (at your feet).

Ball Hawk - Someone usually close to the ball, in the right place at the right time, and a person who specializes in scoring rebounds.

Bat - The bone (hardest portion) of your foot.

Bent/Curved Shot - A shot that spins and curves as it goes towards the net. This shot is used when you need to shoot around defenders or goalkeepers. Though you use the bone of your foot to strike the ball instead of following through the ball with your entire body, you end up just following through with your leg and cross your legs as you are shooting the ball.

Bicycle Kick ("Overhead Kick") - where the ball is above you and you proceed to jump up and kick the ball while the ball is in the air.

Broom - In this book, it is the area on your foot towards your toes. There is space in your shoe between your toes where there is a lot more fabric and a lot less bone, which makes it a soft area on your foot, similar to the softness of a broom.

Champions League - The UEFA Champions League is an annual soccer competition involving the best of the best club teams from many of the countries in Europe.

Chop - This is performed with the outside of your foot. The leg that is cutting the ball must step entirely past the ball. Then, allow the ball to hit that leg/foot, which effectively stops the ball. Having the ball stop next to your foot enables the ball to be pushed in a different direction quickly.

Crossbar Challenge - Played by one or more people where you attempt to hit the crossbar by shooting the ball from the 18-yard box.

Cruyff - Cut the ball, but leave yourself between the defender and the ball. In essence, you are cutting the ball behind your plant leg.

Cut - This is performed with the inside of your foot. The leg that is cutting the ball must step entirely past the ball. Then, allow the ball to hit that leg/foot, which effectively stops the ball. Having the ball stop next to your foot enables the ball to be pushed in a different direction quickly. Additionally, you may cut the ball so that it is immediately moving in the direction that you want to go.

Driven Shot - A shot struck with the bone of your foot, where you follow through your shot with your entire body without crossing your leg. This is the most powerful type of shot.

Counter Attack ("Fast Break") - When the team defending gains possession of the ball and quickly travels up the field with the objective of taking a quick shot, while few of the other team's players are able to travel back to defend in time.

Finishing - The purpose of shooting, which is to score.

Flick - Barely touching the ball to change the direction of the ball slightly for a teammate when a pass is being played to you.

Half-Volley - Striking the ball just after it hit the ground, but while the ball is still in the air.

Jab Step ("Feint," "Body Feint," "Fake," "Fake and Take," or "Shoulder Drop") - When you pretend to push the ball in one direction, but purposely miss, then plant with the foot that you missed the ball with to push the ball in the other direction.

Jockeying - When defending, backpedaling to maintain proper position in relation to the person attacking with the ball. When jockeying, the defender does not dive in for the ball. He or she waits for the ideal time to steal the ball or poke it away.

Jump Turn - Instead of pulling the ball back with the bottom of your foot, as you would do in the V pull back, stop the ball with the bottom of your foot as you jump past the ball, landing with both feet at the same time on the other side of the ball. Landing with both feet at the same time on the other side of the ball allows you to explode away in the direction from which you came.

Offside - When you pass the ball to a player on your team that is past the opposing team's last defender. You cannot be offside on a throw-in or when you are on your half of the field.

One-Time Shot - When a pass or cross is played to you and your first touch is a shot on net.

Opposite Foot - Your non-dominant foot. Out of your two feet, it is the one that you are not as comfortable using.

Outside of the Foot Shot ("Trivela") - Shooting with the bone of your foot where your toe is pointed down and in. The ball makes contact with the outside portion/bone of your foot. This shot is useful because it is quicker than a driven shot, it can provide bend like a bent shot, and is more powerful than a pass shot.

Pass Fake - Faking a pass. Keep your form the same as when you pass, including: 1) Looking at a teammate before you do a pass fake 2) Raise your passing leg high enough behind your body, so that an opponent believes you are going to kick the ball.

Pass Shot ("Finesse Shot") - A shot on the net using the inside of your foot. However, land past the ball to increase the shot's power, which is similar to a shot taken with the bone of your foot.

Passing Lane - An area on the field where a teammate can pass you the ball directly, while the ball remains on the ground.

Pitch - A soccer field.

Rainbow - When you place one foot in front of the ball and the laces of the other foot behind the ball. Pin the ball between your feet and flick the ball up behind your body and over your head.

Roll ("Rollover") - Using the bottom of the toes of your foot, roll the ball parallel to the defender, crossing your feet when you plant. Then, bring your other foot around to uncross your feet and push the ball forward. The path the ball takes is the shape of an "L."

Self-Pass ("L," "Iniesta," or "La Croqueta") - Passing the ball from one foot to the other while running. Imagine you are doing a roll, but without your foot going on top of the ball. Instead, it is an inside of the foot pass from one foot and an inside of the foot push up the field with the other foot.

Set Piece ("Dead Ball") - A practiced plan used when the ball goes out of bounds or a foul is committed to put the ball back into play. The most common set pieces are throw-ins and free kicks.

Scissor - When the foot closest to the ball goes around the ball as you are attacking in a game. Emphasize turning your hips to fake the defender. To easily turn your hips, plant past the ball with your foot that is not going around the ball so that you can use the momentum of the moving ball to your advantage.

Shielding - Placing your body between the ball and the defender. With your back facing the defender and your arms wide, prevent him or her from traveling to the ball.

Shot Fake - Faking a shot. Make sure your form looks the same as when you shoot, including: 1) Looking at the goal before you do a shot fake 2) Arms out 3) Raise your shooting leg high enough behind your body, so it looks like you are going to shoot.

Square to your Teammate - Pointing your hips at a teammate.

Step On Step Out - In order to change direction, step on the ball with the bottom of your foot. Then, with the same foot that stepped on the ball, take another step to plant to the side of the ball, so that your other leg can come through and push the ball in a different direction.

Step Over - When you are next to the ball and you have your furthest leg from the ball step over the ball, so your entire body turns as if you are going in a completely different direction. The step over is best used along a sideline.

Through Ball/Run - When a pass is played into space in front of you, allowing you to continue your forward momentum.

Toe Poke/Toe Blow - Striking the ball with your big toe. The toe poke is the quickest shot, but often the most inaccurate shot.

Upper 90 - Either of the top corners on a net (corners are 90 degrees).

V Pull Back - Pull the ball backward using the bottom of your foot. Then, use your other leg to push the ball and accelerate forward in the other direction, hence the "V" in the V pull back.

Volley - Striking the ball out of the air before it hits the ground.

Wall Passing ("1-2 Passing") - A wall pass is where you pass it to a teammate and they pass it back to you with one touch similar to if you were to pass a ball against a wall.

Acknowledgments

I would like to thank you, the reader. I am grateful to provide you value and to help you on your journey of becoming a more confident soccer player, coach, or parent. I am happy to serve you and thank you for the opportunity to do so. Also, I would like to recognize people that have made a difference and have paved the way for me to share this book with you:

First, I want to thank my mother who has been a role model for what can be done when you work hard towards your goals. Her work ethic and ability to overcome adversity are truly admirable, and I look up to her for this. Also, I appreciate her feedback on wording and grammatical improvements.

Second, I would like to thank the content editors Kevin Solorio, Paul Marvar, Tom Catalano, Toni Sinistaj, and Youssef Hodroj. They reviewed this book for areas that could be improved and additional insights to share. Without their input, this book would not be the high-quality reading material you have come to expect in the Understand Soccer Series.

Lastly, I would like to thank my soccer trainer, Aaron Byrd, whose wisdom and smarts have turned me into the player I am today. His guidance and knowledge about this game have made it so that I can pass this knowledge on to rising stars, coaches looking to grow their understanding of soccer, and caring parents!

Many thanks,

Dylan Joseph

What's Next?

Each of the chapters in this book aims to increase your ability to successfully pass to a teammate or receive a pass that increases your chances of scoring. Implementing the tips, tricks, tweaks, and techniques you just read in this book will surely help you in achieving your dreams to become an outstanding soccer player. If you enjoyed the contents of this book, please visit my website at UnderstandSoccer.com to let me know what you were most excited to read.

I aim to create a book on nearly every topic covered in the first book in the series *Soccer Training: A Step-by-Step Guide on 14 Topics for Intelligent Soccer Players, Coaches, and Parents* and would love for you to answer the **one question poll** at UnderstandSoccer.com/poll to help me determine what area of soccer you want to improve next. The fifth book in the series will be *Soccer Defending: A Step-by-Step Guide on How to Prevent the Other Team from Scoring*. However, your vote on the upcoming books in the series will help determine what book is to follow!

15060288R00062

Printed in Great Britain
by Amazon